Cultural Change
Through
Measurable Management

Cultural Change Through Measurable Management

Robin Byrne

ISBN 978-0-557-09253-6

Contents

Foreword

One day a few years ago I was working in my office when I got a telephone call from someone with a funny accent who told me his name was Robin Byrne. It took me a minute to figure out he had something to sell me, and I don't remember exactly what he was saying but for some reason I stayed on the line with him, which is not typically how I handle unsolicited calls from sales people. I do remember having the impression that this wasn't just a salesperson, that the man had a certain authority about him and sincerity in what he was saying that transcended what I would expect. And pretty soon I became very interested in what he was talking about – something he was calling Measurable Management™.

As a leadership consultant myself, what Robin was saying about Measurable ManagementTM couldn't have been more relevant for me in my work. For me, he was giving me the missing link I had been looking for in my work: the bridge between my own initial focus with clients (creating the foundation for being successful in some organization-wide initiative or strategic implementation) and being successful at the implementation of what got created in that period I call formulation. What I heard – and have a much more refined view and respect for in the years that followed – was that Measurable ManagementTM was both a methodology for training people at any level to be better leaders and better implementers and a way to change the culture of the company in the process.

Hence the title, "*Cultural Change Through Measurable Management*".

Since then, there have been many telephone conversations, meetings, collaborative thinking and design sessions, and even a few beers. I got to know Robin pretty well, including both the light and fun-loving side of him and the more serious brilliance of his business and process side. Robin's colleague, Denny Bixenman, came to a course that I give to consultants to learn how to do some of the kind of work that I do, and I came to a course Robin and Denny give to consultants to license them in the kind of work Measurable Management™ does. Robin and I were both speakers at a Lean Conference in Tulsa, and we had dinner together with Dr. Jeffrey Liker, a professor at the University of Michigan's College of Engineering and author of *The Toyota Way*. During dinner we discussed and agreed on the importance of getting alignment and changing cultures to ensure the success of both Lean and Six Sigma initiatives. Since my focus has been on gaining executive team alignment to propel a company forward in the fulfillment toward their aspirations, the common theme and oft-reinforced conclusion has been how perfect a fit there was between Robin's work and my own.

Lastly, the main thing I can tell you is that Robin knows his stuff and has a lot to offer. When I participated in his course that I mentioned earlier – in Las Vegas, of all places – I met and interacted with a bunch of consultants who have led Measurable Management™ programs inside of organizations of all kinds and sizes, and their level of commitment and enthusiasm was inspiring.

Welcome to Robin's book and Robin's world. Glean from it all that you can. It'll be worth the effort.

Miles Kierson
President, KiersonConsulting
Author, *"The Transformational Power of Executive Team Alignment"*

Author's Comments

A word of advice to the reader:

This is not a very long book and you could probably sit and read the whole thing in about an hour. My advice is that you read a chapter or maybe two chapters and think about the content and then read that same chapter or two a second time and then put the book down. The next day, read a little more, think about it and read it again and so on. Spread the book over two or three days and soak in it rather than take a quick shower. These pauses for thought and repetition will have a much deeper effect on you than the quick blast and this will enhance the chances of you reacting to the content and perhaps behaving differently as a result. It's much like washing your car by hand rather than putting it through the car wash, at the end you still have a clean car but the hand wash has helped you to identify blemishes and other areas of detail that you might not otherwise have noticed and that you may want to fix.

Furthermore if someone in the future asks you if you have read "Cultural Change Through Measurable Management" by Robin Byrne you'll be able to reply by saying "Actually I've read it twice" and if nothing else, this makes me look good.

Measurable Management™ is something that I developed out of my experience as a manager with Xerox in the UK. It is delivered by a facilitator to groups of Team Leaders in all kinds of organizations and as a result change happens, cultural change and measurable improvements to whatever you're trying to measure and improve.

I often get asked if it's like Lean or Six Sigma. If it were Lean, it would be skeletal and if it were Six Sigma it would be a V6 with twin turbo chargers. The organizers of the 2008 Lean Summit in Tulsa Oklahoma described it as, "unnervingly simple yet powerfully effective, the missing link". I recently visited a Measurable Management™ program being implemented within the US Air Force and heard a very seasoned Sergeant describe it as "the most effective program for making things happen that he had ever experienced". I simply describe it as a practical vehicle for implementing strategy and delivering results.

This book is not the Measurable Management™ program it is simply an explanation of what Measurable Management™ is and how and why it works. I am confident however that there is much that you can borrow from the book and put into practice. I sincerely hope that you find it both interesting and valuable and I thank you for picking it up and reading this far.

www.measurablemanagement.com

Chapter One

Cultural Change - What Is it?

We often hear talk of changing the culture of an organization but what does that mean? What exactly is the culture of an organization?

It's really quite simple. The culture of an organization is about the people who work for it, how they behave in order to achieve their business goals and satisfy customers. The culture of an organization shows itself in how people communicate, how they make decisions, how they treat each other and how they treat their customers and suppliers. It can be measured in how quickly people are able to identify a problem or an opportunity and then respond to it and deliver a successful outcome. In other words it affects the organizations ability to change in order to meet the needs of their customers. Talking to customers is crucial to developing a culture that can respond to change.

A friend of mine told me the following story that is reportedly true.

A sweet grandmother telephoned St. Joseph's Hospital. She timidly asked, 'Is it possible to speak to someone who can tell me how a patient is doing?' The operator said, 'I'll be glad to help, dear. What's the name and room number?' The grandmother in her weak, tremulous voice said, 'Norma Findlay Room 302.' The operator replied, 'Let me place you on hold while I check with her Nurse After a few minutes, the operator returned to the phone and said, 'Oh, I have good news. Her nurse just told me that Norma is doing very well. Her blood pressure is fine, her blood work just came back as normal and her physician, Dr. Cohen, has scheduled her to be discharged on Tuesday.' The grandmother said, 'Thank you. That's wonderful! I was so worried! God bless you for the good news.' The operator replied, 'You're more than welcome. Is Norma your daughter?' The grandmother said, 'No, I'm Norma Findlay in 302. No one tells me s#!t.

Whether it's true or not it's funny and it makes the point that we should never miss an opportunity to talk to our customers. Even handling a complaint is an opportunity to talk with the customer and show them that you care and that you want to do a good job for them. Remember that customers tell four times as many people the bad news than they tell the good news. Listening to our customers gives us a head start over competitors that focus on their products. When the market shifts the product focused company struggles to change and meet the new expectations of the customer.

Organizations that struggle with change basically have a problem with culture. In these organizations negativity, fear and internal politics are easily identified and these elements conspire to strangle change initiatives and improvement projects.

I remember working with a newspaper publisher in the UK who had many cultural issues. When mistakes in advertisements were made the advertising sales department blamed the art department and the art department blamed the sales department. While they continued to blame each other the quality of their work did not improve and mistakes continued to happen and customers were upset. Additionally there was little or no cooperation between the editorial department and the advertising department. Opportunities were lost as journalists wrote articles focusing on a variety of issues that could have had advertising opportunity linked to them if only they had given advertising sales a heads up. Lost revenues, lost tempers and lost customers as a culture of blame and internal politics conspired to stifle innovation, miss opportunities and build resistance to change.

The culture of an organization directly affects the health of the organization. It affects the agility and speed at which it can respond to change. The role of leadership therefore should really be to develop a healthy culture in order to shape a healthy future for the organization, a culture where people ***work in association with one another, not in conflict***, a culture that involves people and respects their contribution. Unfortunately many organizations are still managed by leaders who craft solutions to problems in the dark of night and then impose their solutions on the workforce. These leaders feel that their role is to develop solutions to problems and then show people how to implement these solutions. Is it any wonder that they meet with resistance to change when the ownership of the solution is resting with the leader and not resting with the people charged with implementing it, the workforce?

I remember a meeting in the nineties with the Managing Director of a very large chain of copy and print shops in the UK. They were the first big chain in the copy shop business in the UK and their franchise sales grew very rapidly. After explaining my views on leadership and the importance of involving others he told me that it would never work in his company "I make the decisions and then I tell them what to do and if they don't do it they're in big trouble". Needless to say as competition became fierce they struggled to retain their number one position and his management team bought him out. My very first boss from my days at Xerox became a director of the copy shop company and as the culture shifted towards involvement they halted the decline and remain a major player in the market.

The involvement of others can also be referred to as "Engaging the Workforce" and the health of the organization is directly affected by how engaged the workforce is.

How healthy is your organization? Who makes decisions? Who's involved? Who implements? Who is talking to the customer? The answers to these simple questions are the difference between a culture that embraces change with enthusiasm and a culture that resists it.

While Lean and Six Sigma are excellent tools for process improvement they are weak culture changing initiatives. They focus on the technical side of process improvement and they forget about the people and how these changes will affect them. I listened to a manager from Toyota speaking at the Lean Summit in Tulsa Oklahoma. He said that people visit the Toyota plant and comment that they use the same improvement tools in their companies that Toyota are using but "Why is it that Toyota's results are so much better than ours"? He went on to say that what they don't see as they walk around the plant, is the culture of the organization. They see the flow charts and the Ishikawa Fishbone diagrams and all the statistical process control charts but what they can't see is the attitude of the workforce. Dr Jeffrey Liker, author of the Toyota Way once told me over dinner that Toyota successfully changed their culture but it took them 10 years to do so and they couldn't really tell you how they did it. Leadership somehow forced it to happen.

Changing the culture of the organization shouldn't take 10 years, so how do we do it more quickly?

Having identified a set of objectives to be achieved, we need to focus on how people behave, how they communicate and how they treat each other and their customers in order to achieve those objectives. We need to develop a listening and involving style of leadership, a style that encourages input from the workforce. One of my core beliefs is that *the best consultants any organization can have already work for it*. By encouraging leaders to ask questions and listen to the workforce you begin to develop a "Pull Style" of leadership a style that taps into the expertise that already exists within the organization and begins to unleash the change potential of the workforce.

This approach can work on its own or alongside other existing initiatives like Lean and Six Sigma, *working in association with one another, not in conflict*. Rather than displacing or disrupting other initiatives you could describe it as like adding a supercharger to the process improvement engine.

It's obviously not that simple or Toyota would have not taken ten years to change their culture. Well actually it may not be that simple but neither is it really all that difficult. By taking a structured approach to developing a Pull Style of leadership you can start to see a significant change in people's attitudes and behavior in as little as 6 to 12 weeks.

Measurable Management™ provides such a structured approach and even if you don't go down the route of implementing a Measurable Management™ program in your organization, this book will provide you with awareness of some of the things that you can do to bring about cultural change within your organization.

Chapter Two

Measurable Outcomes

Business Leaders today spend a significant amount of time and energy crafting the strategies and direction that their companies should take, but communicating that vision and implementing that strategy is no easy task.

Have you ever spent money on a training course or a quality improvement initiative for one or more of your people? It may have been a one day workshop or a lengthy program that ultimately led to a recognized qualification or it may have been a *"free"* seminar. Even the free ones cost you money if you put a value on the time invested and the drop in workplace productivity. Of course we see training our people as a necessary and valuable investment and most would not argue against that view. We spend time and money on development in order that we may reap the benefits of improved performance in the workplace.

How much return on investment did your organization achieve from its training expenditure last year? Many of you reading this will not know the answer to that question but will comfort yourselves by saying something along the lines of "I'm not certain how much return we got but I'm sure it was substantial". Organizations know what the ROI is on their pension schemes and their plant and machinery so why not on their training and development?

Part of the problem lies in the way that organizations handle training and development. Not surprisingly Human Resource departments focus on the people in an organization. They carry out a training needs analysis and identify the strengths and weaknesses of personnel and put together development programs aimed at strengthening those weaknesses. Focusing on the individual and especially focusing on the weaknesses of the individual is a fundamentally flawed approach.

In order to measure the return on the training investment we need to focus on the needs of the business and not the needs of the individual. We need to focus on what the individual can do for the organization and not what the organization can do for the individual. When we offer employment to individuals we do so expecting them add value to our organization and we compensate them financially and with other benefits in return for their labor, their skills, their experience, their enthusiasm and their creativity. We interview people and we give them a job when we recognize one or more of these qualities so it would make sense to concentrate on tapping into these qualities.

Instead of performing a training needs analysis we should perform a Business Needs Analysis. What improvements from an organizational development viewpoint do we want to see as a direct result of investing the organization's money into training and development, quality and continual improvement?

Learning must deliver real and measurable outcomes into the workplace that meet the needs of the organization, the department and the individual and it should do it in that order.

Most organizations are not philanthropic bodies that exist to do nice things for the workforce; they exist to satisfy their customers, achieve their objectives, their key business issues and to do this efficiently and profitably. This is the very essence of being a quality company in today's highly competitive business environment. Organizations have to identify and meet the needs of the marketplace more effectively than their competitors if they are going to retain customer loyalty and this inevitably means developing a culture where employees must become customer focused and embrace the continual improvement philosophy. Initiating change within the workplace should be and must be a natural part of daily working life. This requires significant cultural change for many organizations. Changing the way people think and act is no easy task.

The change that has to happen in order to have the most impact on the customer will happen not at management level but at operator level within the day-to-day processes whether they be manufacturing products or developing services, sales and marketing processes, patient care in hospitals, administration, distribution or research and development. The people with their hands on these processes are not the managers they are the workforce and they are working in the present. They are coming in and taking care of today's tasks in order to meet today's deadlines.

The management team is hopefully looking toward the future. They are coming up with Vision, Mission Strategy, Policy and all that other sexy stuff but fundamentally all that they are saying is, "This is where we are today and this is where we are trying to get to in the future". In order to get there, things need to change. Organizations today generally realize that if they don't initiate change they will not thrive and they may not survive. The challenge is in making change happen at the sharp end, at the process level. **This is where the wealth is created in the organization** and this is where the customer is ultimately engaged and satisfied or otherwise. You can make changes all day long at management level but it is a complete and utter waste of time unless the changes that you make there are driving significant change at operational level.

My Father turned 90 years old in May 2009. He gave up driving his car when he was about 83 I think. The deciding factor was the day that he drove into town to get his grocery shopping and then returned home on the bus. When he looked in the garage later that day and there was no car inside and he thought it had been stolen. He'd forgotten that he'd left it in town. I remember laughing when he told me the story but he commented that it wasn't funny because it was the second time he'd done it. It reminded me somewhat of the story of the man who said " I want to die like my father, peacefully in his sleep .... unlike his passengers who were screaming in terror". Thankfully my Dad had the good sense to realize that maybe now was the time to change before something more serious happened and he now makes full use of his senior citizen bus pass.

I think my Dad sets a really good example to us all. How many organizations have made the mistake of not recognizing the need to change? They only respond when they are backed into a corner or when something bad happens and often by then it's far too late. Change should ideally be proactive not reactive although it is impossible to foresee everything and therefore agility to react to the unexpected is also essential.

The managers who are closest to these operational processes are our supervisors, team leaders, first line managers, cell leaders and leading hands. This level of management is the "linchpin" within the organization between its objectives and the outcomes. They are the bridge between your visualized future and the people that will get you there.

This is the level of leadership that will translate all of the good intentions of the board room, into real and measurable results at the sharp end. It is right and fitting therefore to make this level of management the focus of training and development in order to empower and equip team leaders to handle the problems of initiating change within the organization.

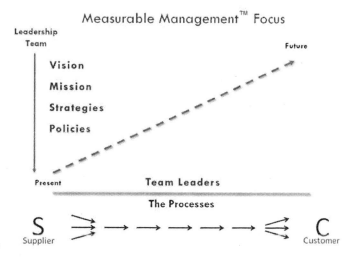

Many organizations recognize the situation of when having invested in training and developing their people, they return from the course or workshop exclaiming things like "It was excellent! The best course I've ever been on!" and then they slip behind their desks or machines and continue to do things in exactly the same way as they did before. All we have to show for the investment usually is a certificate or something similar that tells us that they successfully completed the course. We're left to think "They must be better at what they do because they successfully completed the course so we must be getting a benefit", meanwhile questions are being asked of us such as "How are we performing against our targets?" "What are the customer satisfaction figures like?" "How much revenue have we generated this month?"

Most managers would like to see the training investment deliver an instant measurable return within the issues which are important to them and against which they themselves are being measured. It therefore makes sense to start a development program with a Business Needs Analysis rather than a Training Needs Analysis of individuals. This subtle difference puts the focus onto the organization and its needs rather than on to the individual. This is a large piece of the philosophy behind Measurable Management™. The success of Measurable Management™ is measured by how well the participants have translated the good intentions of the board room into measurable improvements within the Key Business Issues that are relevant to their organization. When they are using the skills for leadership and the tools for quality introduced by the program to deliver measurable improvements within these vital few business issues, then the training will have delivered a visible benefit into the organization and a tangible return on investment will result immediately. How do you know that you are improving if you can't measure it?

Setting the direction for change is vital but organizations will inevitably meet with resistance from the workforce if there is not a culture that embraces change. Resistance is natural, embracing change is not. Changing attitudes is necessary, shifting ownership of problems and their solutions is essential to a smooth implementation of improvement ideas.

Measurable Management™ changes attitudes. Measurable Management™ brings about Cultural Change.

Let's find out how!

Chapter Three

Key Issues

In order to initiate change into an organization you need direction, call it targets, goals or strategic objectives, vision, mission or anything that is meaningful to you. This is the domain of the Senior Management Team. Retreats, Strategic Planning sessions, Gap Analysis, SWOT Analysis, Benchmarking and many other popular approaches are very commonplace.

The outcomes from these approaches result in Vision and Mission Statements, Strategic Objectives and occasionally action plans that are supposed to make it all happen. Basically all that is happening here is a process that allows the management team to identify where they are now from either a business or organizational perspective and where they'd like to be in a timescale from now. That timescale usually covers anything from twelve months to five or even ten years.

The sad reality is that all too often Mission Statements get hung on walls in reception to impress visitors and business plans gather dust on shelves.

A friend of mine Miles Kierson the author of "The Transformational Power of Executive Team Alignment" once said to me that the word "team" often has no place in the phrase "Management Team". He describes the management team as "a group of people who get together for meetings and then go back to getting on with their own agendas within their own departments".

In my experience Senior Management can usually tell you what Key Issues are facing their organization without needing a retreat to think it through. When I start the Measurable Management™ process in an organization I usually ask senior management this very simple question. "If you could wave a magic wand over your organization, where would you like to see real and measurable improvements in the next six months? It's very important to have only two or three Key Issues and certainly no more than four because you cannot change the entire world in six months so think carefully about the Key Issues that would really put a smile on your face if you could deliver valuable improvement into those areas".

These two or three issues will then become the success criteria against which you will measure your achievements and from an action planning point of view is really about as far as you need to go as a senior management team. Remember what we said earlier? "The best consultants that an organization could have already work for it". If the senior management team develop an action plan and then try to impose it on the organization, **it will meet with resistance**.

The implementation has always been the most important and simultaneously the most neglected part of organizational development. There are countless consultants that will help you to develop your strategy but there are precious few who are prepared to roll up their sleeves and get into the trenches with you to facilitate execution. Why? It's simple; they don't want to be accountable for the outcomes. It's too easy for them to help you with the strategy and then walk away. If you struggle with the implementation they can say "We did our job but the client failed to do what we told them".

Implementation is much harder than strategic planning because you have to get it done through others. Ultimately whatever you plan has to be put into practice by those who have their hands on the day to day processes that produce the outcomes. It's harder because the larger the organization is the further away from the processes the senior management are. Like a game of Chinese Whispers the message is handed down from on high and is in danger of being gradually corrupted so that by the time it gets to the workforce the accuracy of the original message is lost. So how do you pass the responsibility for implementation to the workforce? Let the workforce develop the implementation plan. Reduce the risk of a corrupted message.

Look to your Team Leaders, your Supervisors, your First Line Managers or whatever job title you have given them according to what kind of organization you are. These people are the most important layer of the management structure as far as implementation is concerned. Those individuals with their foot on the first rung of the management ladder are *"the linchpin"* between all of the good intentions of the boardroom and the people who will get you there, the workforce.

There is much debate about whether improvement initiatives should start top down or bottom up. I really think it doesn't matter too much as long as they start and for me Team Leader or First Line Manager is the logical place. This first level of management will bridge the gap between your envisioned future and the people that will get you there.

These are the people to give the key issues to because they are the closest to those who have their hands on the everyday processes. This is where the wealth is created in an organization and through these everyday processes the customer is ultimately engaged and either satisfied or dissatisfied depending on how good the organization is.

It is worth reinforcing at this point that **developing the culture first is vital**. Don't fall into the trap of instantly focusing effort and finance into process improvement in order to satisfy the customer. Lean and Six Sigma make this mistake and although they achieve good outcomes they would be significantly better if training in leadership and teamwork were not bolted on later as an afterthought. Keep a tight rein and hold back on process improvement until the cultural foundations are laid. **If you develop a customer focused culture you will not be able to stop the process improvements from coming through.** This desired state is the antithesis of planning improvements and then trying to overcome resistance in order to implement change. We will discuss more on how to develop this culture but for now let's stay with our Key Issues and return to cultural change at the appropriate time.

Having decided on your key issues you don't need to worry too much about whether or not they are the right issues. Usually they are but occasionally you may be wearing your blinders and not see something important or you may simply get your priorities wrong. Have no fear because if you did not get it perfect your workforce "the best consultants you could have" will soon identify and bring to your attention other issues that may become more of a priority. If they are right then show your agility to redefine the issues remembering to keep them to just two or three.

Now you need to focus your Team Leaders onto these issues and this is where middle managers or department heads become involved in the process. The Team Leader should meet with their immediate manager with the Key Issues as the focus for their discussion and answer a few simple questions:-

- How do the organization's Key Issues impact on our department?
- Where do we see opportunities for our department to make a contribution towards achieving improvements in these areas?
- How will we measure these improvements? Will it be in areas such as budgets met, sales increased, fewer complaints, reduced rework, reduced scrap, increased productivity, improved efficiency, repeat

business, improved margins and any other areas pertinent to your organization and your customers?

The answers to these simple questions define how you will measure your success. How the Team Leaders answer the third question will define their personal success criteria. This is the first step in aligning the workforce behind your Key Issues and ensures that the language of the boardroom is translated to the language of the workforce. Improved cost control translates into less scrap and fewer mistakes.

Organizational alignment from top to bottom is highly desired but not 100% essential to making a start. My aforementioned friend Miles Kierson, expert in Executive Team Alignment will cringe at this but as much as I would love to have a perfectly aligned Executive Team and the entire workforce aligned behind them I am happy initially with getting as many people looking in the same direction as possible and steadily turning more heads as we gather forward momentum.

So having set the direction and pointed the heads of all those "Linchpin Leaders" in that direction, you are ready to proceed with laying the cultural foundation for change to happen within these Key Issues.

Chapter Four

Thinking, Feeling and Willing

Perhaps the most obvious difference between being a leader and being a non-leader is the reliance on getting things done through other people. This can be reliance on direct reports or on people in other departments. It becomes more complex when some of those people in other departments are actually positioned higher in the company hierarchy than you are. This poses a real problem because you will only be effective as a leader when you have the necessary skills to motivate, instruct, support, develop and communicate with others. It is from within this skill set that the organization's culture is shaped. **It is from within this skill set that truly outstanding leaders emerge**.

Since strangling is not an option how do you influence behavior?

Understanding people and knowing how to win their cooperation is just as, if not more, important as understanding the equipment, the products and the processes. This will help develop the teamwork that is necessary for project implementation. It will add value and momentum to any existing initiatives such as Lean and Six Sigma.

Working in association with others is clearly more productive than working in conflict. Conflict is the enemy to good associative and productive relationships. Imagine any of the relationships in your life, personal or professional as being a straight line reaching to infinity in both directions. The further you travel in one direction the stronger the association grows and the further you travel in the opposite direction you move away from association and closer to conflict. We constantly move back and forth along this line in each of our relationships. One minute things seem to be going well and we are moving toward association then something irritates us or offends us and we retreat towards conflict. These movements are sometimes very small and almost unnoticeable but even so, we need to make a conscious effort to move towards association. Even if the steps are very small they are at least steps in the right direction.

It is important at this point for me to draw some distinction between positive conflict and negative conflict. Positive conflict is represented by healthy disagreement or differing opinions that result in healthy discussion leading to improved outcomes. Positive conflict actually encourages working in association so that both parties agree to the improved outcome. On the other hand negative conflict is represented by rude, aggressive and disruptive behavior that creates friction, hostility and disharmony. When we say that conflict is the enemy to good associative relationships we are clearly referring to negative conflict. It is the responsibility of the leaders in the organization to minimize and eliminate negative conflict. Leaders need to recognize that in order to develop good teamwork we must recognize that **Conflict** is our enemy and overcoming or avoiding conflict in the first instance is the key to working in association with people and creating the foundation for a positive culture

This is basic common sense. When you discuss this topic with your people at any level in your organization they will nod their heads in knowing agreement then carry on behaving in the same ways that they have always done. You have to do something to make others change their behavior and this is the challenging part. It's not enough knowing what to do because without repetitive opportunity to behave differently you will not change your own behavior or the behavior of others. You can't change the perceptions, attitudes and behavior of others after only one try but you can do it pretty quickly through action, reflection, learning and repetition. Repetition is the key.

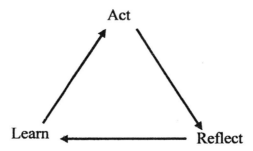

So what repeated behavior can make others behave in a positive way? We need to know this before we can act on it, reflect on our actions, learn from that and repeat by doing it better.

The answer lies in human nature and this next model helps us understand what we need to do.

The Thinking Feeling Willing Model

There are many theories about how people's minds work and what their motives are but it is generally accepted that we tend to operate on three levels: the Thinking, Feeling, and Willing levels and that we move between these levels constantly and sometimes very rapidly. It is probably safe to assume that as you read this you are operating on the Thinking level:

On the **Thinking** level we absorb information; we process facts, receive, digest, and communicate information. This information can be received by any of our senses and will trigger a reaction within us. It may be an impulse to act, to respond or it may simply be a feeling.

On the **Feeling** level we react to people, events and information. We experience moods and emotions such as happiness, sadness, liking, disliking, anxiety, humor, and anger. These feelings usually trigger our actions. How we feel about something influences how motivated we are to react in either a positive or negative way.

On the **Willing** level people are motivated (or de-motivated). They commit themselves to an action, they work towards an aim, they make an effort.

Our friend in bed here takes in some information on the **Thinking** level. The alarm clock is telling him it is time to get up. There may be some other information however that we cannot see… His nose may be telling him how cold the room is and his feet may be telling him how warm the bed is. On the **Thinking** level therefore all of this information tells him it is time to get up but quite naturally on the **Feeling** level he doesn't feel like he wants to. His reaction on the **Willing** level therefore is to lie there a little longer. Eventually on the **Thinking** level he receives more information, i.e., it is now a few minutes later. On the **Feeling** level he may become worried about possibly being late for work and getting into trouble. This feeling triggers off his **Willing** level and he becomes motivated to rush and dress in order to avoid trouble by being late.

As human beings we operate on these three levels constantly and jump rapidly in fractions of a second sometimes back and forth from one level to another.

Simply put, on the thinking level we are exposed to something and the nature of what we are exposed to triggers our feelings which in turn triggers our behavior. How we are exposed to it is the key to our behavior. If a waiter is friendly we feel good and give a good tip, if the waiter pays little attention to us we feel unimportant and we reduce the size of the tip.

If you want the workforce to behave positively towards you, you have to influence them in a positive way on the thinking level and create a positive perception of you in their minds. This positive perception creates a positive attitude on the feeling level and positive behavior on the willing level.

Chapter Five

Perceptions, Attitudes and Behavior

Look at this model and see how Thinking, Feeling, and Willing is translated into Perceptions, Attitudes and Behavior. On the Thinking level our Perceptions are formed, on the Feeling level our Attitudes are formed and this influences on the Willing level our visible Behavior.

The information received ultimately influences the actions of the recipient in a way which is decided by how positive he or she feels about that information. It is essential to feed information in a positive manner to create positive feelings and therefore positive action.

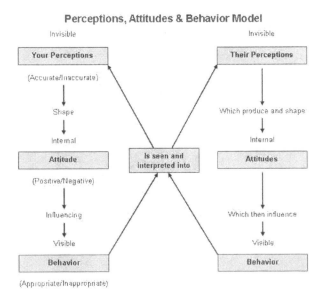

Perceptions, Attitudes & Behavior Model

The only part of this process that you are in control of is your own behavior. If you want to change or influence the way others behave, you only need to think about how to behave in a way that will improve their perception of you. Once you have achieved an improvement in their perception of you (thinking) their attitude (feeling) towards you also improves and so does their behavior (willing). They have no choice in this; it follows as naturally as night follows day. So what single piece of behavior can a leader demonstrate that will have the biggest impact on positively influencing people's perceptions of them?

You can discover the answer by asking a group of your people to complete a simple exercise. Ask them to think of a manager or supervisor that they perceive to be a good manager. Choose a real person that made you feel that he or she were good at leading others. Ask them to write down what it was about the behavior of that person that made them think he or she were good at leadership.

Then get them to do the same exercise but ask them to think about a poor leader. Think about a real person that they felt was not good and managing, supervising or leading and write down the behaviors of this individual that created this perception.

In almost every case you will find consistent comments about the good manager that imply good listening skills. They will write things like He/She was always interested in my opinion. His/Her door was always open. He/She listened to what I had to say. He/She asked for solutions. He/She asked for my input. He/She was a good listener.

In contrast the bad manager has behaviors that suggest the opposite. There is nothing there to suggest good listening and involving skills.

The answer is therefore very clear and very simple. If we demonstrate listening behavior to others we influence their perceptions of us on the thinking level dramatically. You can actually be very weak in many other areas of leadership but your team will still perceive you to be a good leader if they perceive you to be a good listener. It's basic human nature. As human beings we like to be listened to, we warm towards those who show interest in us, it makes us feel valued. Those who are poor listeners annoy us with their interruptions; irritate us with their lack of attention brow beat us with their own ideas and proposals. On the thinking level we see them as aggressive, authoritarian, more interested in their own opinions than in our ideas. On the thinking level we become uncomfortable and resist their ideas. On the willing level motivation is usually low, people resent the changes, there is a high risk of conflict. **Conflict is the enemy to good associative relationships that develop a positive culture.**

This is how the perception, attitudes and behavior model works, your behavior influences the behavior of others and simply by making a conscious effort to show that you were listening to someone you will have a significant influence on their behavior.

Now at this point you may be metaphorically nodding your head in agreement but when you are confronted in real life with an opportunity to either give your opinion and offer a solution or to ask a question and listen to your co-worker, what will you do? In my experience through the Measurable Management™ program most people start to offer their opinions and ideas rather than inviting the ideas and opinions of others. This is why Act, Reflect, Learn and Repeat is necessary. If we recognize our Push Style behavior and learn to change it to the Pull Style then the more we repeat those Pull Style behaviors they start to become second nature. We start to replace actions that create conflict and resistance with listening behaviors that motivate and encourage teamwork.

It takes practice to make a conscious effort to show people that you are listening to them. It's not enough to just listen, you have make the effort to show them that you have listened. You have to practice behaviors that are more for their benefit than your own, paraphrasing what they said, commenting on how strongly they appear to feel about an issue shows them that you listened. When you do this you instantly reduce conflict levels and create very positive perceptions.

I was watching TV in England one evening when an advertisement for Army recruits came on the TV and caught my attention. The camera represented the eyes of the Army officer as he approached an angry group of rebels with his patrol. The rebel leader looked like a ruthless individual and he shouted and yelled waving his automatic weapon as the British Officer approached. The voiceover commentary asked "If you were this officer, how would you get this man to share his water with you and your troop"? At that moment the officer removed his sunglasses and the commentary continued with "making eye contact is the first step in showing that you are listening to someone and reducing conflict levels".

The point is that it is hard for people to maintain their anger and aggression when they recognize that you are listening to them. You may only reduce the conflict a fraction but even a fraction is a movement away from conflict and towards association. Remember our imaginary relationship line? The moment the rebel saw that the officer was preparing to listen (thinking), he felt less threatened by him (feeling) and he started to behave less erratically (willing). The officer was in control of his own behavior and he avoided the knee jerk reaction to respond to aggression with more aggression.

Behavior really does beget behavior and if someone shows negative behavior toward you it is only human nature to want to respond to them with negativity. A smart leader however learns to overcome their instinctive response and meets negative behavior with positive behavior. Listening is positive!

One who is skilled in listening techniques and asks questions rather than gives opinions becomes a very strong influencer. It is possible to influence the behavior of more senior personnel and get their cooperation by employing these very same techniques that you would use with your own direct reports. Indeed you may not have any direct reports at all but by using this approach you can gain the cooperation of anyone.

Although Pull Style is preferred there are times when it is inappropriate and using the Push Style is necessary. Such occasions usually occur when time is against you and you don't have the luxury of discussion opportunity. Our Army officer will use a Push Style if he and his troops come under fire. In an emergency situation you give orders and instructions and you expect your people to do as you wish. The more you

Pull people in non emergency situations the easier it is to Push them when the situation demands it. You must therefore be confident using both styles but its interesting and somewhat comforting to know that by getting good at Pull Style makes it easier to Push when you have to.

At this point you might be thinking "What does this have to do with the Key Issues that we set out earlier"? Good thinking I'm glad you brought it up and stopped me from going off at a tangent.

Chapter Six

Resources, Relationships and Processes

The key issues are the areas where you would like to see measurable outcomes. If you are going to develop a listening and involving style of leadership then you need to use your new powers of influence over others to deliver the measurable outcomes into your key issues, your success criteria.

If you want to achieve that success you only have to do three things. These are the three things that everyone does in order to deliver a successful outcome to any situation whether it be in our personal lives or our business lives. In order to achieve a successful outcome you:-

1) Manage the resources that you have at your disposal.
2) Manage the relationships between those who are essential to getting it done the ones that make it happen.
3) Manage the process that makes it happen.

If something goes wrong and you get an unplanned or unexpected outcome and you are able to identify what caused that outcome, you will always find that the root cause sits in one or more of these three areas. There really is nowhere else for it to sit. This is what you do when you manage any situation, manage the resources, manage the relationships and control the processes.

Your organization may be a manufacturing company, or a not for profit charity, a fire department, a city government or an insurance company. It makes no difference because whatever type of organization you are, in order for you to do whatever it is that you do, to deliver your goods or your services you always need to manage your resources, manage your relationships and control your process. This is the very essence of Measurable Management™. Listening to and involving your people as they identify which resources, which relationships and which processes are in need of improvement. You begin to tap in to their expertise and as they take ownership of problem areas you start to see attitudes beginning to change.

Try another simple exercise either with the same Team Leaders that you did the Good Manager/Bad Manager exercise with or try it with a different group.

Ask each of them to write down the name of a resource that they or their team use on a daily basis. It could be a tool, a machine a document with important information or anything.

Then ask them to write down what people do when they use this resource; in other words ask them to describe the process.

Finally ask them to think about the people involved in the process and how they relate to each other and write down any words or short phrases that come to mind. Is there, for example, an atmosphere of mutual understanding and trust, or one of suspicion and hostility in their relationships with others? Simply get them to write down the words that they think describe the relationship conditions in which they work.

When you review their responses it is easy to see how Resources, Relationships and Processes come together to affect the outcome of an activity.

When you review their responses you should do this with your organizations Key Issues in mind.

Firstly you might ask each individual how satisfied they a the resource that they listed. Some will be satisfied and others will have issues. They may think a particular tool is perfect for the job but they don't have enough of them. If they are less than satisfied with the resource then you need to know why, you need to know how it affects them and how it affects the outcome. Is there a negative effect on either the organization or the customer caused by this resource issue and does it impact on any of the key business issues? If it does it will most likely need addressing and will become the focal point of some kind of improvement action.

Then turn to the processes that they described. Do they always run smoothly without problems? What goes wrong? Who is affected when it goes wrong? What is the impact on the organization or the customer? Does it affect any of the Key Issues? If there are problems within these processes and Key Issues are affected then these processes may also become the focal point of some kind of improvement action.

Finally look at the words used to describe the relationship conditions. Do any of the words or phrases have negative connotations? What behaviors created these perceptions? Is it behavior that you would like to change? Is it having a negative impact on any of the Key Issues? Might there be more improvement actions.

A simple exercise such as this can highlight numerous resources, relationships and processes that if improved will have a positive and measurable impact on your Key Issues but you don't have to jump in and do anything about it right away unless health and safety is an issue. You may just record the problem and think about who is affected by it. Perhaps these people would be the best people to involve in crafting the solution? It is an important part of changing the culture to identify who has to implement the change and offer them the problem rather than crafting your own solution and giving it to them. When people craft their own solutions they take ownership and implementation is executed with more enthusiasm than if it were imposed on them.

Up to now we have talked a lot about managing relationships. You have learned that conflict is the enemy to good associative relationships and that listening is the ally.

With our processes it is complexity that is the enemy and teamwork is the ally in overcoming complexity. We will talk about this in much more depth later in chapter nine.

That only leaves resources....

You may have many resources available to you such as tools, machines, vehicles, money, energy, services and the list goes on. The truth however is that your two most important resources are your people and the information that you have. You can actually outperform your competitors who may have better equipment and better facilities than you if your people are motivated and if you are better informed than your competitor. **People and information are unquestionably your two most valuable resources**. There are many sporting analogies to prove this statement. We have seen David and Goliath stories in sporting contests many many times. The underdog defeats the favorite because they only get this one big chance, it means more to them that it means to the superstars who have played in many finals so the underdog is more motivated. Also the underdog may have a player on their team who is now in the twilight of his career and may have played for the competition, so he knows about his ex team-mates and their old injuries and weaknesses that you and your team can play to. On the day, the motivation and the knowledge about the other team combine to produce a victory.

Listening is the golden key to everything. When we listen we motivate people and obtain information. Listening is therefore strengthening our two most valuable resources. When you coach, counsel or appraise your people remember that this is an opportunity to have a meaningful conversation. A conversation perhaps where you do more listening than talking.

Chapter Seven

Coaching, Counseling and Appraisal

If you are to manage people and influence positive behavior, you need to evaluate how your people perform and give them constructive feedback. You also need to know how you are performing yourself as a leader. You should therefore seek feedback on your own performance in order to develop yourself as a leader.

Not surprisingly, the same listening skills that help us create positive perceptions and influence the behavior of others are also the fundamental skills that will assist us in giving and receiving feedback.

By now you should realize that a leader's job is to shape the culture of the organization, a culture that will allow you to implement change through other people. We have begun to look at establishing good foundations through active listening to begin this process. Taking this to the next level we need to look at not merely implementing change but taking responsibility for initiating change and sharing that responsibility with others.

Everyone in the organization is capable and responsible for identifying improvement opportunities. By using and developing your active listening skills in coaching, counseling and appraisal situations you can continue to inspire, motivate and develop your team while giving them an opportunity to share their ideas with you. The more you ask questions and listen to the answers the more you strengthen your two key resources of people and information.

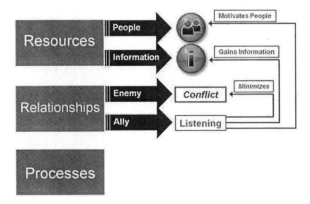

This book is not going to try and teach you how to improve your coaching skills. This book is not the Measurable Management™ program, it is simply trying to help you understand how Measurable Management™ works and lets you try to put it into practice in your own way. Measurable Management™ doesn't give you answers and tell you to do things in a particular way. It helps you to look at your present situation and to generate ideas and plan your own solutions, improve performance, learn and develop from real experience.

Wait a minute, isn't that the same as coaching?

Absolutely! You're really getting the hang of this stuff.
When you are coaching you focus on two things:-

1. Improved Performance
2. Learning & Development

As a coach you are concerned with how immediate aspects of work are performed and you aim to help your team member develop their own solution to improve it. At the same time you are aware that the team member may then be better able to solve the next problem more independently.

By encouraging them to play the maximum part in improving their performance, offering support through thoughtful questions and tentative suggestions you try to give the team member the right mix of direction and choice. This will mean that they are neither over directed nor immobilized by having too many options. This approach of exploring the problem together, working in association enables the team member to develop new knowledge, skills and competencies for future problem solving opportunities. More importantly it encourages a change in culture by being the type of leader that others can look to and model themselves upon. This is the type of good leader that your people will think of when they do the Good Manager/Bad Manager exercise, always interested in them and their opinions, always encouraging and giving praise and recognition for jobs well done.

They will copy your behaviors; copy your leadership style model themselves on you. As any practitioner of Neuro Linguistic Programming (NLP) will tell you and as we have already shown you in Perceptions, Attitudes and Behavior, Behavior begets Behavior. It's like viral marketing via the internet. Your behavior influences others and their replication of your behavior influences many more. You show your team members a listening and involving style as you coach and counsel them and they in turn show their people the same. Culture changing behavior.

This approach not only delivers powerful results but you get something out of it too. You get the immense satisfaction that comes from developing others to become "self-motivated" developers themselves.

In setting out to make improvements you need to remember that the key to being a successful Leader and Coach is to constantly learn from experience. Whatever actions you take, always be prepared to review what you've done and seek feedback from your team, learn from this review, and then plan for the future on the basis of what you've learned. Don't forget the Learning Triangle from chapter three! Practice! Practice! Practice!

Formal appraisal meetings should be conducted in the same way. Obviously there is the formality of documentation that needs to be completed but remember what we said at the end of the last chapter, an appraisal is an opportunity to have a meaningful conversation. A conversation perhaps where you do more listening than talking.

I was taught that in an appraisal, the emphasis should be on the praise part of the word. After starting the meeting in a relaxed way perhaps over coffee, start by complimenting or praising your team member on anything at all that they do well. Nobody is bad at everything, find something that they are good at and praise them so you build up a kind of positive credit balance rather than plunging them into the red. I picked up that last analogy from a training video by Video Arts the company founded by John Cleese of Monty Python fame. That video encourages you to ask the individual to share with you what else they think they are good at and suggests that you should agree with them if you think it's appropriate to do so thereby building an even more positive credit balance. Do you see what's happening here? Of course you do you're quick learner.

Your positive behavior and your questions are creating a positive **perception** of you. This is creating a positive **attitude** in the mind of the team member and their **behavior** as a result is more relaxed and they become more open and talkative which in turn allows you to do more listening. Asking "which areas do you think you need to improve in?" is much more positive than forcing your own opinions onto them about where they need to improve. Ownership is being placed with the individual creating motivation and reducing resistance.

There are books and training videos and all kinds of courses on how to do appraisals some good and some not so good. All I'm trying to do here is show you how to apply the "Pull Style" to the appraisal situation. If you want someone to improve in a certain area, that improvement will be ten times more likely to happen if you can get the individual to tell you that they are weak in that area and if you can get them to decide on the actions to be taken to improve. It's more likely to happen because ownership of the problem and the solution sits with the person who needs to implement it. If you tell them what's bad and what you want them to do about it the ownership sits with you and they are less motivated to remedy the problem.

The structure of the Measurable Management™ Program allows you to try out these techniques and reinforces these behaviors through work-based activity that apply what you have been reading and learning to the specifics of your job. The coaching, counseling and appraisal activities are done with the key issues in mind. You are encouraged to focus on performance improvements that are directly relevant to one or more of these key issues.

In more of the words of John Cleese and Monty Python ....“And now for something completely different”!

Chapter Eight

Trust Me! Ask Nelson Mandella

You can do this Pull Style stuff… Trust Me!
It's easy…Trust Me!
It really works… Trust Me!

In 1997 I was invited to speak at the Graduate Institute of Management & Technology in Johannesburg, South Africa. I was the guest of Andy Andrews the then director of GIMT and I was exposed to some of the most opulent boardrooms I'd ever been inside. These were very wealthy companies and I was suitably impressed by the furniture and the décor as well as the almost Royal treatment that a guru such as me attracts. In reality I was only getting an audience with these captains of South African industry because of Andy Andrews. They didn't know me from Adam but they knew Andy Andrews and more importantly they trusted Andy not to waste their time with frivolous meetings. Years of listening to these people, working with them and following through on his promises had developed their trust in him to deliver what he promised and in Measurable Management™ he was promising results more powerful than anything else that they had ever experienced from GIMT before.

As a result of my presentations and their trust in Andy Andrews, the national electricity company Eskom and Siemens South Africa decided to implement Measurable Management™ and I returned in 1998 to train 24 facilitators to run the programs.

Trust is a valuable commodity. It's hard to gain but so very easy to lose. You are not going to trust me because of anything I say to you, you are only going to trust me by how I behave toward you. Your trust in me is developed in your perception of me and rooted in my behavior toward you. The truth is you are unlikely to ever trust me personally because I only get to speak to you through this book, I don't get to follow through with actions that support my words. If someone that you trust recommends me to you then perhaps your perception of me will be influenced and you may become just a little more trusting of me.

This is how it works in real life. You demonstrate your trustworthiness to one person and they can influence others. Just like that viral marketing stuff we mentioned earlier.

As part of their training we took the 24 South African facilitators through the same games and group exercises that they will take Measurable Management™ participants through to embed these behaviors. One of these group exercises is called Reds and Blues. It's a very simple exercise that begins by splitting the group of Measurable Management™ participants into two teams. The objective of the exercise is for your team to end with a positive score. It's not a competition to beat the other team and outscore them but the fact that we used the word teams instills the idea of competition into many of the participants. That word has already for some of them influenced their perception of the purpose of the exercise and will inevitably influence their behavior.

The details of the game are not important suffice to say that points are awarded to each team and are determined by the choice of color that each team makes over a period of ten rounds. In each round the teams make their choices and points are awarded accordingly. If they are astute they quickly realize that beating the other team is not part of the agenda. They simply have to end up with a positive score and Red is the friendly color. If both teams play reds in each round, they both consistently gain 3 points and both end up positive. Win/Win.

After round 4 the teams get an opportunity to communicate with each other by having one representative from each team get together for two minutes to discuss anything. In South Africa I observed a lady from one team meet with a gentleman from the other team. The lady's team was leading with a positive score and the man's team was trailing behind and in a negative situation. He proposed that both teams play red from there on and both teams would end up in a positive position. It didn't matter who had the most points as long as they both ended with a positive score. She agreed and shook hands and they returned to their respective groups to report back on the agreement and then move forward.

On hearing of the agreement that she had made and that she had shook hands and given her word, her male colleagues realized that the lamb was ready for the slaughter and decided to overrule the agreement and play a blue. This would give them an even higher positive score and plunge the other team even deeper into negativity. Despite her protests the others went ahead and in protest she took no further part in the exercise because they had made her appear dishonest. Not only could the other team no longer trust these guys but even their own team member no longer trusted them. As a result war broke out and blue became the color of choice. Trust had left the building and an eye for an eye was the order of the day. With each round of the exercise the volume in the room rose and so did the level of conflict. The end result was an inevitable lose/lose with neither side ending on a positive score.

Conflict is the enemy to good associative relationships listening is the ally. They had heard this message several times but when the opportunity arose they reverted to type and let the competitive nature of human beings take over, thus demonstrating the challenge of trying to change the culture of an organization. This exercise proved to be a turning point however and the penny dropped for the participants. The next exercise was almost 100% teamwork.

On a return visit to Andy Andrews' home he showed me a book. It was Nelson Mandella's autobiography with a personalized message written inside to Andy. It said "Thank you for all that you have done toward the economic development of South Africa" and was signed Nelson Mandella. Andy held the book open at the personalized message, looked me in the eye and said "That's Measurable Management™". I'm sure that GIMT and Andy Andrews were the ones responsible for Mr Mandella's gratitude but I also like to think that Measurable Management™ made a contribution and deserves a little of the credit.

Trust is essential if you are going to change the culture of an organization. In chapter one I wrote "Organizations that struggle with change basically have a problem with culture. In these organizations negativity, fear and internal politics are easily identified and these elements conspire to strangle change initiatives and improvement projects" How can trust exist in an organization such as this, filled with negativity, fear and internal politics?

Trust is a natural bi product of a Pull Style of leadership. Listen, support, encourage and deliver on your promises and you will be perceived as a trustworthy leader.

Trust me I know what I'm saying, ask Nelson Mandella.

Chapter Nine

A Rut and A Grave

The way that an organization operates and develops is not only affected by the people who own and work for that organization, but also by its customers and suppliers. It is essential to consider the vital role played by customers and suppliers—both outside and inside the organization—and the relationship between them. This relationship is at the heart of all business activity and is one which leaders need to be constantly aware of when embarking on a change program of improving resources, relationships, and processes.

A quality organization is one that is customer focused and aware that the needs of the customer are always changing. Organizations that fail to respond to those changing needs are effectively "standing still" and will be caught, overtaken and left behind by their competitors.

Not to improve is fatal. Organizations who fail to respond to changes in the marketplace become stuck in a rut of "product focused production" and the **only difference between a rut and a grave is the depth**.

As a child growing up in working class Northern England I lived about half a mile from a factory that manufactured TV sets. The company was called "Redifusion" and was a popular brand name in the seventies. A neighbor who worked there boasted that only one in a hundred of the TV sets that they made failed to work first time and required some rework before it passed inspection. He felt that a 99% success rate was pretty high and in those days it probably was. At the same time however Hitachi and Panasonic were saying to their respective workforces that it was important to push the bar higher and have only one TV in a thousand fail. When they achieved that they pushed for one in ten thousand and then parts per million. By the time Redifusion and others in the industry awoke to what was happening their products were more expensive than the competition because of costly rework and obviously less reliable due to lack of quality improvement. The Redifusion factory is still there but now it manufactures Ebac dehumidifiers.

In this example it was simply failing to improve that forced Redifusion out of business. Not listening to the customer can have the same effect, we only need look at the British and American automobile industries to find numerous examples of failure to compete due to a product focused culture as opposed to a customer focused culture.

In considering your organization's customers you may identify different groups, all with very different needs. In some organizations this is not a problem, a car manufacturer, for example can respond to these different needs by manufacturing a wide range of models. What would a hotel do though when faced with some customers who want nightlife on the premises and others who want peace and quiet?

This illustrates a very important point about customers—their needs may not only differ but may actually be in conflict with each other. This may lead to the organization having to decide that one group of customers is "prime" and that their needs take priority over others. In this way the organization begins to identify its primary market.

Successful organizations are those that really pay attention to meeting their customers' needs. Everyone has a part to play in this, either directly or indirectly, as any suggestions that you make for improving the quality of goods or services, or for increasing the efficiency with which they are produced or supplied, will have an impact on your external customers.

By constantly bearing in mind the needs of your external customers, you will in fact be "marketing" your organization. In a very real sense that's what marketing is about. It's not just about advertising, or conferences, or special offers (although these may well be important aspects of selling merchandise), it's about bearing in mind the requirements of the external customer at all times, finding out who those customers are and what they require, measuring the extent to which you are meeting those requirements, and trying at all times to do even better at meeting those requirements.

Measurable Management™ helps you to focus on the customer through simple straightforward work based activity and constantly evaluates the outcomes of these activities with the Key Issues in mind. How can problems or opportunities to improve customer satisfaction be defined in terms of resources, relationships and processes? What key issue is it relevant to? Who will be affected by the outcome or be required to implement the changes? Who needs to be involved in developing a solution?

Always try to look at what you do through the eyes of the customer and not through the eyes of the workforce. I once asked the workers in a struggling carpet factory to describe what their organization does. I asked them to write it down and then to share their answers. The manufacturing department said "We make the finest Wilton and Axminster carpets in the world". The design department said "we create the finest Wilton and

Axminster carpets". The sales department said "We sell the finest Wilton.....
etc". Each department said almost the same thing but each clearly saw it
from their own department's point of view. If they had asked the customer
the same question they would most likely have heard a different response.
Perhaps they would have heard "They make expensive carpets", or "I hear
their designs are old fashioned", or "You have to order well in advance so
as not to be kept waiting".

Less successful companies are "introverted", that is they see
everything in terms of activities or what they themselves are interested in
doing or producing. They are stuck in that rut of product focused production
with the business graveyard fast approaching.

Quality and continuous improvement has been around for a
long time now and everyone should know by now that we have internal
customers and suppliers as well as external customers and suppliers. Each
of your internal customers is the next link in a chain between you and
the external customer, and you should treat them both as customers and
as partners in a program of continual improvement if you are to meet the
needs of the external customer.

Of course, as with external customers, it's not always easy to
identify the needs of your internal customers and their requirements often
conflict with each other. However, finding out who they are and what they
need can shed light on the things that are going well and that should be
maintained, as well as on matters that are not going well and should be
changed. Remember that if something is not as it should be the solution
will always be a resource, relationship or process adjustment or overhaul,
so breakdown the problem into discussions about these areas and let the
internal customers and suppliers develop the solution themselves.

You're probably thinking that it sounds way too easy for it to really
work well. I assure you that with practice it is that easy, Trust me! Ask
Nelson. All you need to do is give them some basic but highly effective
tools.

Chapter Ten

The Hammer

Measurable Management™ keeps it simple. There are lots of tools available for controlling processes and some of them are quite complex and almost require a degree in mathematics to be able to understand them. I'm pretty sure that Michael Angelo used a hammer and chisel to sculpt his Statue Of David. Would it have been as great a work of art if he'd had CAD CAM design software electronically linked to a machine to carve it out for him? I think not. The simple tools allowed him to create a masterpiece.

It doesn't have to be complicated. You can deliver outstanding improvements with two very basic tools. Let's take a new approach to flowcharts and fishbone diagrams and see how these hammer and chisel devices can not only improve processes but develop teamwork at the same time.

Let's begin by explaining what we mean by a process. A process is simply a series of actions that follow on from one another to achieve a desired outcome.
Example: Getting a can of pop from a vending machine:

Step 1 Read the instructions on the front of the machine to establish the cost of the drink.

Step 2 Take the money from your pocket or purse and select the correct coins.

Step 3 Insert the coins into the coin slot on the front of the machine.

Step 4 Read the number allocated to your choice of drink from the list on the front of the machine.

Step 5 Type the number of your selection using the key pad on the front of the machine.

Step 6 Press the vend button.

Step 7 Remove your drink from the dispenser below.

Step 8 Collect any change you may have from the change dispenser.

Everything we do at work is part of a process of some description. Even answering a call is a process on its own or could be part of the order-taking process or the customer complaints process. Entering details into a computer could form part of the invoicing process or the distribution process. It could be part of the sales process if we are recording account details. Sometimes the outcome of a process is not what we were expecting, it is an undesired outcome. The root cause of this unplanned outcome will always be a resource problem, a relationship problem, a process problem or a combination of two or more of these areas. There really is nowhere else for the problem to sit.

If you did not get the can of pop that you wanted perhaps you did not have the correct coins? (Resource) Perhaps you relied on someone else to get it for you? (Relationship) Perhaps you simply pressed the wrong button? (Process). Perhaps you left your change in the machine? (Just plain stupid).

Joking aside, this really is pretty easy stuff and definitely not rocket science.

It's important to remember to think of everything that you get involved in at work as a process.

Drawing a flowchart of the process that you want to improve is a great beginning but let's apply what we have learned. From a Measurable Management™ perspective the process must be relevant to one or more of the Key Issues. Why spend time on improving a process that is not a priority to the organization? This is an important consideration. By applying this criteria you can deliver dozens of measurable improvements into your two or three key issues in a matter of weeks in a controlled and focused manner.

Who needs to be involved? If more than one person puts their hands on this process you must involve them. If there are too many then you must at least involve some of them and let everyone know what's going on. Don't try and impose your opinion of what the flowchart should look like. If they are not involved then they won't feel engaged and because of their lack of ownership they will resist the change. (Perception, Attitudes & Behavior)

Agree on the planned outcome. Ask everyone what the desired outcome of the process should be before you start drawing the flowchart. This is the same as identifying the needs of the customer first. Just getting everyone who handles this process to agree on the precise outcome can instantly improve results and reduce variations in quality. Not all operators have the same quality standard. If they agree a precise definition of the outcome and they stand by it then no customer internal or external will be disappointed with the outcome.

Agree on the first step. Ask everyone to say what they think is the first step. You may find that there are differing opinions so don't record the first step until your team has agreed on it. Again you must avoid giving your opinion. The role of the leader here is simply to facilitate the expertise from the team members.

Repeat this action for each step of the process until you reach the outcome.

Record these steps in a series of boxes that represent the ideal process and detail each step like the example here of the flowchart of a stamping process.

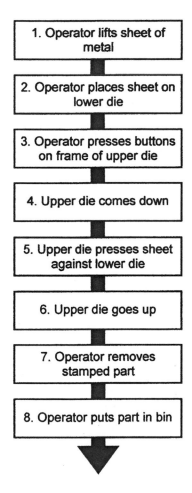

This single line flowchart is the process as it would occur every single time if nothing at all went wrong.

Of course we have not finished because whatever the process might be, the team will look at it and their own experience will instantly tell them that it doesn't always go smoothly. Sometimes or even frequently things do go wrong. The ideal process is one thing and the reality is another.

In the stamping process the team may point out that the machine frequently jams and product is thrown into the scrap. Perhaps the hydraulics leak and need frequent refilling. Perhaps the raw material runs out and you have to make a trip to the warehouse for more.

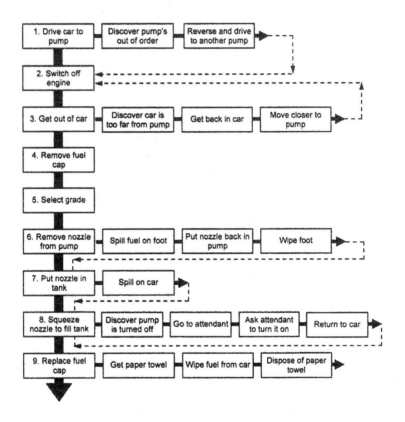

If the flowchart of a process is to help you change and improve that process, it must show the actual as well as the ideal stages. A flowchart of getting fuel for your car may look similar to ours.

It's hard not to conclude that there are often many differences between the ideal stages and actual stages of a process. This points to a tendency in people to think in terms of what should happen rather than what actually does happen. The consequence is that when things go wrong, they end up vaguely wondering "Why?" rather than being ready to deal with the problem.

In chapter five I stated that **complexity** is the enemy to our processes and that we would discuss this in detail in chapter nine. Well this is it.

The column running straight down the left hand side of the chart is the ideal process but the horizontal lines that appear show us where complexity is occurring and causing additional work to be done. Everything to the right of the ideal process is extra work and therefore extra cost and increased inefficiency. The job of the leader is to try and eliminate the horizontal inefficient steps in order to make the process more efficient and cost effective.

It is important to acknowledge that processes can be simultaneously complicated and efficient. By complexity we are referring to re-work or additional work created by inefficiency.

We can use a flowchart therefore for two purposes: 1) We can use it in a traditional way to communicate how something is done, or 2) We can use it to identify where complexity lies in a process.

Any box in the left hand column that has a step to the right coming from it is added complexity. We can tell by looking at any flowchart written in any language exactly where the complexity is just by glancing at it and seeing where the horizontal lines are occurring. A step to the right means complexity.

Complexity means inefficiency, time wasted, resources wasted, added costs, frustration, reduced profit, disappointed customers . . . and on and on!

It is efficient and desirable to move through the process without ever having to step to the right.
The people who operate and run the process should always be involved in drawing the flowchart. This will do several things for you at once:

1. It will sort out any problems that may be occurring because of the differences in the way various individuals run the process. It is

amazing how we think we all do some everyday task in the same way as each other, but when we compare notes we find subtle differences creeping in. Drawing and agreeing the flowchart together irons out those differences and increases the chances of a standardized output.

2.   Through their involvement you ensure that the ownership of the process is with the people performing the activity and the identification of complexity or rework activity is also owned by them. They feel that they are tackling their own problems not someone else's.

3.   You are showing them that you are interested in their opinions thereby strengthening the team spirit. This is the very essence of **teamwork**.

4.   Because you are encouraging their thoughts and opinions you are getting more information on to the table.

It is easy therefore to see how **listening to and involving the team** in a simple flowcharting exercise can not only help you to identify **complexity** but can also avoid **conflict** and strengthen your **people** and **information** resources. This is where having held a tight rein on process improvement until the cultural foundations are in place really starts to pay off.

We have looked at the customer-supplier relationship in terms of you and the processes you are involved in, being the customer. But you are also a supplier, perhaps to both external and internal customers. In the case of the stamping process, the first internal customer is the finishing process, but the main customer is the assembly department.

In the case of a hospital operation, the anesthetist is an internal supplier to the surgeon. The surgeon's customers are the patients. None of these customer supplier relationships will be successful unless they have been efficiently arranged. When looking to improve our processes we should consider any opportunity to involve customers and suppliers of the processes as part of the improvement team. **Teamwork extends beyond our immediate team members.**

Let's assume that we have assembled the right people and that they have successfully flowcharted the ideal process and also included the actual complexities. To begin improving this process by eliminating or reducing complexity as the leader you only have to ask the team.

Ask them which of these loops to the right seem to occur most frequently? Which cause the most problems and create difficulties or conflict? Decide as a team which of these problems is the priority and will benefit the team the most if you can improve it or eliminate it.

Involving them in this decision will increase their motivation to change the process and remove the complexity. When people feel that they the ones that are initiating change, they are not scared or suspicious of it, they embrace it and implement it with little or no resistance.

Chapter Eleven

The Chisel

When you look at the flowchart created by the team, select the stage where you are going to remove complexity and begin to think about what may be the cause of that complexity. Ask the team to choose the stage of the process that they want to improve. They will know which of these rework stages is the biggest pain in the rear. Having chosen the horizontal line of complexity that they want to tackle they need to look upstream in the process from the problem to find the cause and look downstream to see the effect. It is very rare, but not unheard of, for the cause of a problem to be found downstream. The horizontal line of rework is the effect of the problem in terms of having to spend time, energy and money correcting it. If we don't correct it then the effect is an unacceptable outcome that could result in a dissatisfied customer.

To help you look upstream at all of the inputs to the process, a simple but effective tool is the fishbone diagram often referred to as a Cause and Effect diagram. If the flowchart is the hammer then the fishbone is the chisel and when you combine the two together you can create some wonderful results.

A fishbone diagram can be superimposed vertically, on top of your flowchart from the point at which the complexity occurs (see the example).

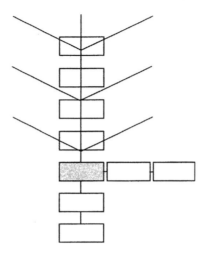

We use the fishbone to look upstream from the point of complexity that we wish to improve and focus on the various inputs to the process up to that point. The cause of the complexity will be somewhere among those inputs. To make it easier we draw the fishbone horizontally and give the different bones some generic headings.

Basic Fishbone Diagram

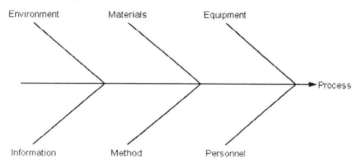

The central feature of the fishbone diagram is a large arrow which represents the process. Leading into this large arrow are smaller arrows, each of which represents one of the main categories of inputs to a process. Typical categories are:

▶ **Equipment**
▶ **Personnel**

▶ **Method**
▶ **Materials**
▶**Environment**
▶**Information**

Simply ask the team to fill in all of the inputs that they can think of under each heading. As they do this human nature will kick in again and they will automatically start to comment and give opinions as to what they think might be the possible causes of complexity and what they might do about them. The leader is using the fishbone rather like a brainstorming exercise and highlights possible causes as they are raised.

Here is an example of a fishbone diagram of a hospital operation. The boxed areas have been highlighted as these are the areas that the team have suggested based on their own experience may hide the root cause of the problem creating the complexity. Participants will say things like. "That air conditioning system is the cause of these infections, I've been saying for years it needs overhauling"! "We should use a different laundry firm for our protective clothing". "The new administrative assistant doesn't understand our requirements".

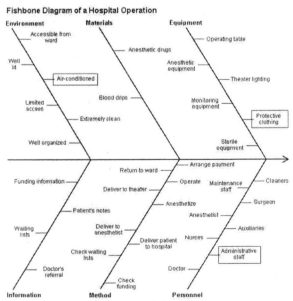

Any of these categories or items has its own fishbone of inputs.

Discuss these opinions and ask them how they would overcome these problems. Who needs to be involved? A volunteer is much more likely to implement the actions than someone who is forced into it so let them tell you what they intend to do about it. If some people are very quiet and not contributing very much, then ask them directly for their thoughts on the problems. Try to see that everyone is involved in some way. The more they take ownership of the solutions the less they will resist the changes that are implemented.

As with the flowchart exercise the role of the leader here is simply to facilitate the completion of the fishbone chart and steer the discussions around the possible causes of problems. Keep your own opinions to yourself. It is important during this process to avoid the temptation of putting your own ideas forward because the ownership will stay with you and not with those who have to implement it.

If the team are struggling to come up with their own ideas and you've tried and tried without success to get them to offer solutions then you may offer your own thoughts. If you do this however and the team show interest in it you must be prepared to hand it over to them. Here is an example of how that may happen:

You say something to the team such as "How do you feel about the air conditioning? Could that be a source of the problem?" This is much better than saying "I think that the air conditioning is to blame". You may get a response along the lines of, "Yes that's a possibility". Whatever the response is, you need to home in on that individual and encourage their input. "Tell me why do you think that Lauren"? You listen to Lauren and then perhaps ask, "Who agrees with Lauren on this?" "What can be done about it"? By now, in a very quick and simple way, you have successfully shifted the ownership of your own air conditioning idea to Lauren and her colleagues who agree with her.

NSK Bearings are a huge international Japanese company manufacturing bearings of all sizes. I remember walking through their Peterlee plant in Northern England and seeing the walls covered in fishbone diagrams and statistical process control run charts. I was about to introduce Measurable Management™ into the company and I wondered if they would think that my hammer and chisel approach was beneath them. I remember one of the participants named Lawrence Sargant telling me that the technique of developing the flowchart in a teamwork situation was something that they had never thought of. Up till then they had only used the flowchart after the change had been developed by the supervisors and the flowchart was used to communicate the new way of doing things to the workforce. They had never thought of using these two tools together like this. I had a similar reaction from Sanyo's microwave division. We wrongly assume that when it comes to continual improvement that the Japanese know everything. **The strength of the Japanese is that they know, that they don't know everything** and they are always looking for better ways. Complacency is fatal.

So we can complete our diagram that we left unfinished earlier by showing that complexity is the enemy to our processes and that teamwork is the ally. Listening to and involving people strengthens our teamwork and through teamwork we can eliminate or reduce complexity.

This chart shows all of the elements of Measurable Management™ that we have been piecing together so far.

Everything we do revolves around our Resources, Relationships and Processes. By addressing the major components of these three areas we enhance our chances of delivering successful outcomes. Simply by doing more listening and involving of others we can impact positively on these major components. Look at the diagram and you can see how listening strengthens our two key resources by motivating our people and getting more information on the table. When we listen to others we reduce the risk of conflict in our relationships with others and build trust. Involving the team in our flowcharting and fishbone diagram exercises uses teamwork to attack the complexity in our processes and transfers ownership of these changes to the workforce.

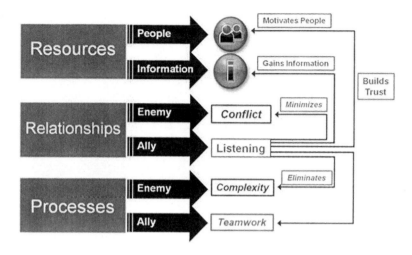

Understanding this is one thing. Implementing it is something else all together. It's time to put all of this good stuff to good use and try implementing these ideas and translating all of these good intentions into real and measurable outcomes. This is where the learning really begins.

Chapter Twelve

Implementation

Having let the team take ownership of the problems and work together to craft the solution you must act quickly on them and don't fall victim to Analysis Paralysis. You can spend so much time debating the who, what, where, when and how that by the time you pull the trigger the target has moved on and it's too late to implement the plan. Sometimes it's simply better to aim and fire then adjust your aim and fire again. It may take more than one attempt but that's much better than leaving it till it's too late to fix.

Make the improvement actions small fixable now ideas that can be addressed in very short timescales. Baby steps are the order of the day. Think of it as doing three or four dress rehearsals before putting on the big show. If you try to implement a major improvement project without these mini rehearsals you risk opening up a can of worms and your team may become demotivated when they can't see the light at the end of the tunnel. Major improvement projects are nothing more than a series of smaller connected actions leading to the desired result. A lot like a flowchart really. So if you really have to change the world in one fell swoop try to break it down into baby steps like a flowchart and implement the steps one at a time in sequence. Your big project becomes several small projects and the team will have confidence in their own abilities to address the bigger picture.

I can't stress enough that these improvement ideas need to be bite-size. They shouldn't take longer than 48 hours to put into effect and it doesn't matter if it only takes 48 minutes. Sometimes an improvement idea can be simply to stop doing something that is a clear waste of time and resources. For example, The Gannett Group are a media giant. They own over 100 newspapers in the USA and Great Britain including "USA Today" as well as over 1000 non daily publications and 23 TV stations. I have worked with them in North of England Newspapers where their Northern Echo publication won the Gannett gold award for best newspaper in the group. One of the activities in the program caused a supervisor to get feedback from the board of directors on a weekly report that he and two of his colleagues spent two hours (6 man hours total) preparing. Each of the five board members told him that they did not use the report for anything but assumed that one or more of the other board members must be using it. His idea for improvement was to stop doing the report. It saved the company over 300 man hours per year and channeled that productivity elsewhere. It was easy to implement.

Sometimes however stopping doing something can be more difficult than it may seem. The US Air Force are trying to implement an improvement by stopping the daily completion of daily audit lists on the thousands of requisitions that are processed every day. The information can be obtained from a variety of other existing documents making the daily audit an unproductive and hugely expensive waste of time and money. The program participant wants to reduce the paperwork and free up tens of thousands of man hours by abolishing this daily audit. Unfortunately the audit is a federal requirement and permission to change it can only come from Washington DC after going through the chain of command. The individual has put in his report and his commanding officer has sanctioned it. If it gets through the chain and is abolished, not only will the US Air Force no longer have to complete this time consuming and meaningless task but also neither will the US Army or the US Navy. It is almost beyond belief how one solitary individual can generate through Measurable Management™ such a small idea with such monumental ramifications and benefit not just their own organization but also others as well as their country.

A Hospital in Iowa made a few simple changes to the process and documentation of insurance pre-authorization and they recaptured over $1.2 million that had been slipping through their fingers every year.

All of these improvements have two things in common. The action required by the team was small and doable in a short timescale and secondly, they were all relevant to their organization's Key Issues.

Remember if it's not clearly relevant to one or more of your key issues you perhaps should choose another process to improve.

Identify a number of improvements that meet the above criteria and decide on how to measure them. Use the measurement criteria that you laid down at the beginning when the Team Leaders sat down with their immediate managers and discussed the impact that the key issues would have on their respective departments. Don't accept justifications like "it will save time" ask them to measure how much time and what is the value of that time in monetary terms? What is the effect on the customer and how much do you lose if you lose the customer? What could be the effect on us if this is a health and safety issue and if we do nothing about it? Can someone be seriously injured? Can we be sued?

Put a time frame on the implementation of no more than a week from the day that you all agreed to do it. Give them two or three weeks following implementation to start measuring the impact of the change that they implemented and then bring everyone together to share the outcomes.

At these presentation of outcomes ensure that the senior management team are there or at least represented by one or more senior managers. If the senior management can't make it, then cancel and reschedule for a time when they can. This is just as important as having the senior managers there at the start when the key issues are discussed and the alignment process begins. They need to hear about these outcomes and they need to give the people who made it all happen the recognition that they richly deserve for delivering real and measurable improvements into the key issues. When they get recognition they want to do another improvement idea. The culture change becomes visible and people start to notice. Mike Widmer the ex Managing Director of Arriva NorthEast Bus once said to me "The financial payback is great but what really excites me is seeing how much their attitudes have changed. Every day they are actively looking for things to improve".

Giving recognition is essential to the culture of a healthy organization. Senior Management must accept that cultural change is just as necessary in the boardroom as it is in the rest of the organization and they must ensure that they are more than a group of guys who just get together for meetings.

Cultural Change through Measurable Management™ is based upon some very simple truths that are easy to understand but can be difficult to implement. Don't be afraid to try and don't be afraid to fail. The more you try to develop a listening and involving style the better you will become at it. Accept that you are not perfect and that self improvement is an important part of cultural change. Look hard at yourself. Don't assume that it's everyone in the organization but you that needs to change. Embrace the opportunity!

The Measurable Management™ program provides a tightly packaged approach to implementing all that you need to do to. I began this book by saying in the author's notes that "This book is not the Measurable Management™ program it is simply an explanation of what Measurable Management™ is and how and why it works. I am confident however that there is much that you can borrow from the book and put into practice". I hope that I was correct. Don't be put off by its simplicity, things don't have to be complex and **always remember to know, that you don't know everything**.